PAPER BIRDS DON'T FLY

Other Works by Al Ortolani

Slow Stirring Spoon (chapbook), High/Coo Press, 1981

The Last Hippie of Camp 50, Woodley Press, 1989

Finding the Edge, Woodley Press, 2011

Wren's House, Coal City Press, 2012

Cooking Chili on the Day of the Dead, Aldrich Press, 2013

Waving Mustard in Surrender, NYQ Books, 2014

Francis Shoots Pool at Chubb's Bar, Spartan Press, 2015

Paper Birds Don't Fly

Poems

Al Ortolani

NYQ Books™

The New York Quarterly Foundation, Inc.
New York, New York

NYQ Books™ is an imprint of The New York Quarterly Foundation, Inc.

The New York Quarterly Foundation, Inc.
P. O. Box 2015
Old Chelsea Station
New York, NY 10113

www.nyq.org

First Edition

Set in New Baskerville

Layout by Raymond P. Hammond

Cover Design by Raymond P. Hammond

Cover Art by Jacque Forsher | www.jacqueforsher.com

Library of Congress Control Number: 2016931046

ISBN: 978-1-63045-026-7

Paper Birds Don't Fly

.

Thank You

The author wishes to express his thanks to the following friends and editors who took the time to be a part of this collection:

To friends and poets, Wayne Bockelman, Amanda Bradley, Tom Burns, Dana Cope, Brian Daldorph, Steve Eichhorn, Francis Ferns, Mike Hogard, Adam Jameson, Melissa Fite Johnson, Gary Grimaldi, Ian Khadan, J.T. Knoll, David McLane, Jackie McLane, Mike Shonk, Robert Stewart, James Tolan, William Trowbridge, Jeanann Verlee, Paige Waldorf, and George Wallace.

To my family, Theresa and Wes Middleton, Karissa and Blane Reeves, Staci Allen, Tyler Allen, Jordan Chapman, Jack Reeves, Ava Middleton, Rider Middleton, Jasper the Cat, and Buddy the Dog.

Thanks again to Jacque Forsher for her artistic talents in supplying the front cover, to Maryfrances Wagner and Alarie Tennille for early advice and proof reading of the manuscript, and to Denise Low, Linda Lerner, Thomas Fucaloro, and Timothy Green for their careful reading and back cover comments.

Special thanks to Raymond Hammond and NYQ Books for their much needed support.

And to my wife, Sherri. who always has my back.

Contents

I. Mickey Mantle as Longshot

III. Returning the Artificial Tree

IV. Paper Birds Don't Fly

Paper Birds Don't Fly

For Deborah Grimaldi, James Ortolani,

Dianna Holman, and Jennifer Tavernaro

I. Mickey Mantle as Longshot

White High Tops

There is a hollow space
under the hedge that we
squirm through, the Smith's
old bitch of a dog growling,
snapping at our heels from
the end of her leash. Billy
Clay is just ahead of me,
his butt so high that it
keeps snagging branches.
The dog strains, grabs
the toe of my Converse.
I kick her in the snout
with my free foot. She
shakes her wooly head,
pulls harder. The shoe
is important to me, new,
a gift on Christmas. Jesus,
I punch Billy Clay
in the ass. He's crying
like a baby. Christ,
I kick the dog three times
in the head. These are
my new shoes. There won't
be another pair until
Easter, if ever. The dog's
grip loosens, only
a shoestring caught in
his upper canine. I shove
Billy with my head
through the hedge. He
smells like piss, blubbering
in the sun, a swollen leaking
inner tube of a boy. The rubber
toe of my left converse
is shredded, even my sock

torn. I slug Billy
in the stomach and
he doubles at the waist.
Look at my shoe, I cry.
My life is ruined.

Original Sin

One of the boys said I'd go to hell
after Sam Sebring and I had dropped
our pants, and in a moment of hilarity
had touched our butts together.
It was the sin of Adam and Eve,
the boy said, being naked outside
in the Sebring's back yard in front
of God and baseball and summer trees.
I'd never heard of such a sin.
I knew about Adam and Eve. I knew
they'd fucked up something fierce. I knew
they walked around wearing nothing
but leaves. Sister Anna, my spiritual advisor,
had only mentioned the apple
of their sin. She'd called it original.
Somehow this made sense of my guilt.
No one I knew went around naked
in the backyard. No one touched butts.
Apple or no apple, it was unique
to the neighborhood. So I asked Wally.
He was at least fourteen,
smoked cigarettes, knew as much
as a magazine on first encounters.
He said original sin was like
a permanent tooth. One day
it just appears, all jagged and pointed,
like a joke, without it you can't chew,
but with it, you do.

Mickey Mantle as Longshot

One night Mike and I blew our allowances
on packs of baseball cards. It paid off. I found
a Mickey Mantle wedged behind the gum. Mike
unwrapped a Roger Maris. We danced in the shade

of the elm behind the concessions. Grimaldi
and Ferns were coming up to bat. We ran
behind the left field fence with about 20 other
Pony Leaguers and waited for the long ball.

A homer, returned to the scorekeeper, earned
a snow cone or two more packs of cards, maybe
a Whitey Ford or a Yogi Berra, maybe a chance
to keep collecting behind the backstop.

With each pitch the crescendo of cicadas rose.
If the ball dropped over the fence, we knew
we were in for a fight. We teased the hitters
with chatter. We chomped our now tasteless gum.

Time hung in the lights like a slow curve.

We Sang Dark Songs in Grade School

All through John
Brown's illness
there was nothing
in the color of his face
but bone, even his tall
sons were scrimshawed
crow's feet.
He rests all winter
in a narrow rope bed
below the stairs, pushed
against the rough hewn
timbers. He must have
cursed the chill
from the river, the lack
of sun in the window.
Under the stairs
that led to the loft, he
listened to the wind,
the ice and snow
creeping into the walls—
the adze edges still
visible today, blades
hacked too deep. Even
years later, long past
his *a-mouldering,* no
softening smooths
the cuts, scars deep
in the white-
washed logs, nothing now
but the song book
and children's voices.

The Fifteen Dollar Vacation

Two teachers on winter break access Netflix
and download all five seasons of *Breaking Bad.*
She makes popcorn and he brings in a 12 pack
from the garage. Somewhere in season two
he lights his father's calabash and stokes it
with the stash he found in the evergreen
across the street. They dim the lights and put the set
on mute. Like kids, they text secret messages
to each other, phones on vibrate. He wakes after
midnight to the wind—tree limbs tapping the siding,
sighing as snow runs the eaves, corners
the chimney. She is still sleeping, the blue throw
pulled up to her chin. The couch is narrow—
the remote control lost in the cushions.

Almost Michael Corleone

Your days as the family hero
are over, your cover
as an English teacher blown.

You've watched *The Godfather*
too many times. Suddenly,
it's you fishing for a pistol

like Michael in the john—Jesus,

the crap you've seen,
and now, smoking a Camel
on the toilet—two Xanax

melting under your tongue
you're not even certain
whose cigarettes these are.

You realize when you walk
back to your plate of veal
you gotta take the shot,

even if it is imaginary—
a movie for god's sake—trouble
needs a bullet in the brain.

Within minutes bad guys
are going to email
your mother the pictures

of everything—the booze,
the porn, the women's shoes,
the impossible stiletto heels.

It's all going down tonight.
Badda-bing, Badda-bang,
Badda-boom.

Popcorn and a Movie

Just before the sun sets, a cardinal
drops into the thickest
tangle in the crabapple. Only
inches from the window, he
balls his feathers to wait out
the night's snow. It is cold, lonely
in twilight. We choose
pay-per-view to ease the passing hour:
popcorn and a movie, a Jack
and Seven, the furnace
in the basement burning.
Yet, we are drawn to the window,
Zero Dark Thirty flickering
in the wavy glass.
The cardinal settles
in his feathers, snow
on his wings—popcorn
in the bowl,
salt on our fingers.

.

Bridge Club

Once a month mom would have to sneak out of the house.
She'd carry her shoes in a sack under her arm

so that our baby brother wouldn't notice she was leaving.
My sister and I were ok with her monthly escape. Dad

cooked boloney and eggs. He gave us each our own
bottle of Dr. Pepper. The key was getting mom out

the front door. She winked at us and we'd run a distraction,
somersaulting, hopping on one leg, singing stupid

baby songs. Mom eased the door shut behind her.
Dad, a stranger to the kitchen, searched for a skillet.

As we got older, mom and dad would slip away together.
They'd leave us in charge of ourselves. Mom would phone

part way through the evening. One evening they left
for a Bridge Club party at the Cope's house.

My sister was first to the phone. She admitted
that she had a black eye and that my brother had run away.

We expected him back when the rain started
because he wasn't wearing a shirt. No, she confessed,

I don't know why he ran away. No, I got the black eye
when my knee hit it. No, I don't know what "related" means.

One time my brother was wrestling with the dog on the floor
and all of a sudden he started screaming and he stood up

with the dog hanging from his nose. My dad swatted
the dog with his bare hand and it tumbled into the living room

where he was never meant to be. He squealed and leapt
into my sister's arms who was rolling on the floor

laughing at my brother. I nearly choked on my spaghetti.
Dad took off his belt and folded it in his hand.

We took my brother in the truck to see Doc Brandt.
He could stitch-up a flap of nose even in his kitchen.

When Mom came home from Bridge Club, we were
all three watching the Flintstones. Dad was on the porch.

Fred and Barney Rubble were locked out of the house
and Dino the dinosaur dog was grinning at them

stupidly from the window. Wilma and Betty were out
and Pebbles was inside, teetering on top of her high chair.

The Lovely Mechanic

After hours, the mechanic
who changed my oil
comes to my house in the icy
night and says she forgot to put
the test plug (not the drain plug)
back in the top of my rear
axle. She holds up
a rachet and a piece of metal
wrapped in a red shop rag.
I'm sorry. I need to put it back
where it should have been.
I didn't notice until you'd gone
it was sitting on the bench.
Didn't you get my phone call?
I left this message you see, but
I'm here anyway to right the wrong
and she crawled under my truck
with a flashlight and a socket,
her legs stranded on the driveway
like those of a corpse, but bent
a little to the right so she could
better see. She kept apologizing
for the screw up, insisting I
come in tomorrow so they could
recheck the fluid level. That's
when she shouted—false alarm. Plug
in place. She wormed from under
the truck back into the cold.
I'm really sorry, she insisted,
for bothering you. It's a plug
of mistaken identity—
she was happy. I was happy,
both of us shivering on the porch
an hour past closing.

Good at What You Do

One January morning, I heard
an unfamiliar scratching in the fireplace,
up behind the iron where the smoke
curls in the flue. I cracked
open the damper and flashed
a light into the darkness. Three pigeons
stared back at me, driven down

by the storm to the smoke shelf.
I used my hand as a launch pad,
swatting them off their perch. I wrapped
a towel around a broomstick
to push them higher. As a final resort,
I grabbed for their legs,
hoping to pull them through the damper

and into the dog's crate.
I finally phoned a professional,
someone good at what he does.
He swept the fire ash into a bucket
and spread a drop cloth
across the rug. He tied a noose
onto a fishing pole, and slowly

eased it into the smoke chamber, the thin
monofilament draping like a necklace.
He wrapped each bird in newspaper
and laid them side by side in a grocery sack.
He stapled the top *click click*
and carried them out to the alley bin,
the bag tapping his leg.

Improvisation

A poet has died. We gather
for a memorial—poems, songs,
anecdotes. We leave images
to hold what's been lost—
to personify what remains.
This morning—rain drums
through the leaves of the maples—
perfect for reading, for leaving one
bulb on in the kitchen
and for keeping the house
as quiet as cedars. Even
the clicking of the computer keys
are muted—doves
in the backyard—three or four
houses away, always in pairs.
If a car should drive the street,
our house appears asleep,
shut for the day, the single light
above the coffee pot
a switch away.

The Ghost Clara

haunts the third floor. We
have waited all night
for her to appear,
wielding Ouija boards, candles,
and polished crystals. She
draws back the curtain
when we leave. Crazy women
see her more than most—she
chases them down the stairs
with her wailing. To others
she is just a floater at the edge
of the eye—we are left with
the sense of being tuned out
of a conversation,
hushed at a party, ears burning,
our sense of belonging
challenged. And that's the thing
about ghosts—they could
tell us so much if they weren't
so inconsiderate, caught up
in their exclusive door
slamming and floor creaking.
Who's to say we won't
meet up later—and then,
there'll be hell to pay.

Reading Fiction after Midnight

After the night shift, my neighbor
rides home on his uncle's Triumph,
seldom climbing out of second,
a warbling hesitation, a caesura
held at the intersection
of California and Sunset.
His Bonneville lapses into silence
two blocks from his house. Frogs
chirr in roadside ditches. Dolly
the terrier yaps across vacant lots.
He sits for a cigarette
at the Yield sign,
wrists relaxed on the handlebars, smoke
like exhaust between his lips. He reads
the road like some read fiction,
given to distance, chilled at bridges,
warmed in bean rows. Sometimes
it is enough for him to sit
with his hand
on the throttle, knowing
he can kick-start
the old motor and drive away.

Steam Engine 1023

Your daughters dig out the sled
and lean it inside the garage, readied
for the overpass at Schlanger Park.
Lamp lit windows hang against
the house like flat screen TV's.
By nightfall, goose feathers loosen
from the clouds and drift in the gray streets.
You step out to the porch and breathe
wood smoke from a neighbor's chimney,
and in the taste of cold
you know today's disappearing, your memories
sculptured in snow. Tomorrow,
a girl with a red scarf flies down the overpass,
her steel runners singing, cutting
towards the chain link. For years
the old locomotive has waited
at the bottom of the hill
for the fastest sleds, daughters like yours
pumping their fists.

Hail Mary

The sycamore is bone
white in winter, the few
straggling leaves like bats,
wings curled, hanging
loosely against the mottled sky.
The jay in the oak
complains of the gray squirrel,
bending limbs, leaping
like a ghost
to connect the branches.
The blue sky is brief. It separates
the clouds—a flotilla
scudding west. The sun
falls between the shadows
of the house. The sycamore
stretches across the walk—
one boney finger to the door,
one hand open to turn the knob.
We are home, plates in the sink,
the television flickering football.
My uncles are a reflection in the end zone,
the family face, the muscle,
the bone, the game clock
ticking through another Thanksgiving.
Johnny Unitas in black high tops
drops into the pocket
to heave a last-ditch prayer
into the lights.

Following Junkyard

My father, as athletic trainer,
let me tag the sidelines
with a small plastic doctor's bag.

He loved the scrappers, tough guys
busting for a fight—my favorite
was Junkyard, Vietnam bound,

half-concussed, fingers tapped
in make-shift splints. As free safety,
Junkyard was the forlorn hope.

Small, but wiry, he launched
his body like a bola, like a sling,
like a helicopter prop.

I followed Junkyard all season

with rolls of tape, nylon-wrapped
smelling salts, and a strange
plastic corkscrew which

when wedged between teeth
could pry open a locked jaw.
Junkyard wasn't far from

joining the punch drunk and
selling popcorn in the stands.
He should have taken up badminton,

miniature golf, or watercolor.
Quit, Dad said, before you feel
as bad as you look. I dropped salt pills

into Junkyard's paw. He winked at me
behind his facemask and grinned
with his toothless, baby-pink gums.

Tony Paces the Sidelines

The word on the street was that Tony
had been a genius, a lawyer maybe,

but scarlet fever had cooked his brain; synapses
had melted into gruel. What was left

kept him shackled, tongue on a spoon
slurping syllables, eyes watery,

rheumatic on game days. He chewed
Union plug, spit on the grass, hands

pocketed with notepads and pencils.
The administration complained about Tony,

a village idiot on the sidelines, ragtag,
unseemly for a conference powerhouse.

He displayed his field pass on a lariat
looping his neck. Each year the same,

coaches planned, posed scenarios,
consulted cigars. Tony paced

the twenty yard line, his flap of brain,
inflamed with offense, moving the chains.

Midlife Crises

For two months I lived in a broken-down bus
behind a friend's house. I went out a lot, especially
when daylight savings time ended and the weather
turned. Mostly, I was miserable. Confident
in little. I kept two lawn chairs outside
the door of the bus. On warm afternoons I entertained
the thought of guests. Like in an intermission,
we'd watch the starlings along the creek bed.
A cemetery bordered the backyard, and as the trees
lost their leaves throughout November,
the marbles became more visible. Often, their slant
would be the last light I saw before sliding the door shut
and igniting the Coleman catalytic, crawling
into my sleeping bag to read Hemingway by flashlight.

One Saturday night after doling bourbon
into a coffee mug, I decided that I'd shivered enough
from dusk to dawn. I borrowed a friend's pistol (an antique
he insisted), and I aimed directly between the headlights.
The wound was anti-climactic, a small dent
next to the VW emblem, no sparks, no gaping hole,
just a small crease in the silence.

Martial Arts

The older I become the less I care about battling
traffic on icy mornings. A travel mug
with coffee, a dip of snuff, sport's radio—little helps.
Just yesterday, I took the wrong exit and found
a stoplight I didn't recognize. Pale sedans
emerged from the gloom, headlights haloed,
drivers hunched over cold steering wheels.
I crossed the intersection and followed the ramp
back to the interstate, merging with the commuters,
the Jo Line, the trash trucks I knew—the turn out
where KayDOT stored equipment, mountains
of sand and gravel—a single light. All exits
lead to morning, ice on the windshield,
the rubber wipers slapping little jujitsu hands.

Dog Poet

Just me and the dog Buddy in the house
this morning. I leave the glass door open
so he has free access to the backyard. He

uses it regularly, chew stick in his jaws,
bouncing through the shade, the speckled sun.
When he disappears around the corner

of the house, I know he's up to no good,
nosing the wooden gate, digging through
the hostas, chewing on the green extension

cord that runs the plastic fountain. Buddy
watches the sidewalk, eyes the corner
where the neighbor appears, walking

the bitch Husky. He barks through the pickets,
hopping on his hind legs. If I could tape
a pencil to his right paw, and flatten

a sheet of clean white paper before him,
he'd probably eat them both
with little regard for diction or metaphor.

Jack of All Trades Drives Irene to the Hospital

At midnight, Jack robs the lawn mower
for extra gas, drains the tank, tilts the red can
into the garage light. Wearing

his best flannel shirt for the introduction to come—
he and Irene drive country roads
for fifty miles in the beat up Ford—
past the drag strip, the massage parlor, the state line liquor.
He stops at Chubb's for water.

They run the garden hose into the radiator
and let it fill. Chubb waves good luck, then
more bean fields, more closed signs—
The streets in Joplin are empty, the traffic lights
down Maiden Lane—blink in syncopated yellow.

Jack pats the hood in the parking lot
at Freeman Hospital—the engine block
seeps oil, pings, smokes as it cools.
Wild geese or ducks, he can't tell which,
honk towards Shoal Creek in low clouds.

By dawn, nothing
looks the same; the Missouri oaks
drop leaves like messages.
Only change is permanent.

Irene resting, daughter in pink.

II. Unbroken Design

Unbroken Design

She sits in a half lotus with a fishing
pole on the concrete pier. A small sailboat
tacks the easterly wind. I say a rosary

for a friend who is ill. Across the lake,
dogs run on the sand, their barking is
like the cry of disembodied crows

caught on the wind, loosened
from the hardwoods. At the foot
of the maple, a cicada shell,

split and paper thin, quivers
with each gust. Kites on the far ridge
strain on nylon strings. The spider

stretches the snare of his web
between the holly branch and the dining
shelter. Suspended as if in constant

prayer, the calm geometry
of his web, unbroken and deadly, collects,
gives pause to the long wait.

The Last Farm on 87ᵗʰ Street

A few head of Black Angus stare dumbly at traffic.
At dusk, as the twilight drains behind Taco Bell,
a woman jogs in a reflective suit. The cattle
become silhouettes. Gradually, the night
slips between the house and the barn
like cold, dark silk. Cattails, clumped
at the pond's edge, are swept
by the lights of a semi on the interstate.

This is loneliness—the empty seat of the tractor,
the shed's open door, the winter air
in deepening darkness—nothing
levees the flood of change. A bucket
hangs on the water pump.

The Wind We See

The sunlight falls unabated
through bare limbs—the sky empty,
branches free of birds. Everything tawny
moves in the wind. Even the river,
brown, ferrous, slides over the shoal—
wind caps lapping towards the sluggish
Kaw. A car battery, overturned, cells
open to the river, is wedged in a windfall,
a perfect dumpsite, close to the road,
remote from highway eyes.
South of here—a tractor
plows through an Osage trash heap,
unearthing pot shards, arrowheads,
axe blades. Stone Age decay is slow,
slower than Styrofoam. I leave the battery,
60 month label fluttering at the edge.
Somewhere nearby is Blue Jacket Crossing,
a natural ford, the old pioneer trace.
I search for its limestone shelf—
the wind in the flying leaves.

In Late Winter—the Squirrel

slips from branch to branch, edges
down to the fence, runs the picket,

and disappears behind the toolshed,
tail waving like a flag of truce.

No one steps into the cold today.
Even the light from the front porch

is a joke—an ironic berry
on a frozen limb.

The neighborhood raccoon, burrowed
below the deck, nurses her kits.

The shivering March has sucked
the shine from her coat.

If we could retreat any further
into ourselves, we would surrender

like the hostas, the azaleas,
the wild rose, waiting in the mulch.

Morning of My Daughter's 40th Birthday

The grass along the road is a motion detector, bent
by gravity, burrowed by mice and rabbits. In this
early November rain I walk to my classroom, eyes

trained on the sidewalk, myopic, focused
on the earthworms stretched like pencils on the sidewalk.
Across the parking lot, what remains of natural prairie

has been cornered between two lengths of highway.
The hawk turns on his wing. The cottonwood,
alive with yellow leaves, drops messages

from high school girls into the laps of boys.

Dusting Back the Five Year Old

The ball smacks him on the wrist
As he swings the bat. He turns his back
And cries, the sharpness of the pain
Too much for a five year old. I tell him
To shake it off and pick up the bat
For another swing. His mother says
She will put ice on it instead
And he can call it a night. I step
Out of the picture, forgetting my father's
Voice in my head. Then he drops
The ice and picks up the bat, swinging
It furiously. I smile and throw him
Another rope. He rips a line drive
Right at my head, his mother cheering.

Driving into Lecompton with an Hour to Kill

The town is pressed
into the hillside
like a wildflower
in a history book—
petals creased, colors faded,
stems stretched
into stains. A woman
sits in the spring sun,
a table of children's clothes
flattened for sale beside her.
She waves to my truck—
the door to the Territorial Museum
propped wide with an anvil
of Burlington rail.
The sign on the door
reads *Everything for Sale
All Weekend.* For the
first time today
an answer isn't expected of me—
Daffodils corkscrew up
from forgotten bulbs.
The Kaw laps against
the cottonwoods. As ancient
as the river, rough bark
buds with new green.

Swamp Tour

A girl has opened a can of black olives.
She wears them on the tips of her fingers
like mermaid's purses. She slides them one
by one into her mouth. They are better
than promises, the juice on each fingernail
cool and salty. Between hammocks,
sawgrass sways against the gunnels.
A ray, more shadow than light,
races below them towards the open sea.
Pelicans perch in the high branches
of the mangroves, nonchalant, self-absorbed.
The girl pries up the olive lid. She licks
her fingers, shoves them in like spears.

Taking the ACT in December

High school seniors file in this morning
to take the ACT. They are taught the future
hinges upon a two digit score that will
open doors. It's a cold morning,
the roads covered with ice. The proctor
carries a cup of Starbucks and a stack
of essays to grade. She is young, just
a year or two beyond college herself.
The boys tap their pencils, wondering
if she is the one who will
meet them after the test, after their scores
are compiled, after the doors open. The girls
study her more closely: her boots,
her tights, her layered hair, the way
she shuts off her phone
and drops it—finished into her bag.

Steps

Iced by light mist, the high
school lot reflects the headlights
of the early arrivals—exhaust
snakes from tailpipes, rubber tires
crunch crusts of ice, Jupiter
high in the west, Venus low
in the south, both brilliant
with indifference like
Christmas lights to the blind.
The janitor ministers to thermostats
and salts the stairs as quietly
as a monk. The short bus
labors up the drive. Paras
converge at the side door
and release the hydraulic lift.
The only student is rolled out,
chair balanced at the tip
of the steel edge. A boy, bundled
in a Bronco's parka, legs
wrapped in sweats, waits
to be lowered to the curb,
his Air Jordans bright,
arranged like distant stars.

Kansas as Wine Dark Sea

Sometimes on misty mornings—
I stand as Odysseus at the window,
floating on the roof of a barn.
The pitch is steep so I have to straddle
the peak, each leg planted
by a rubber-soled shoe. I hold
the weathervane, one of the few
original roosters in the county, and
by leaning left or right, I pretend to sail
through waves of fog, lightning rods
trailing behind like untied
ropes from a mast. Pretty much
that's where it ends—a few curtains
of disguise. Chickens rattle through
the open doors. A black snake
muscles below the hay bales.
Penelope teaches Honors English
to ninth graders in Overland Park.
Telemachus, a KU graduate,
has moved to an apartment
near a micro-brew in Waldo.

Forgetting Dante in Third Period

I was reading canto thirty-four to my senior English class.
Virgil was climbing out of circle nine; Dante
slugged toward Purgatory. The storm
that had been building in charcoal clouds
hit the windows—lightning shimmered, thunder banged.
All seven rows turned to watch.
Spines cracked—terza rima flattened. Twenty-seven
copies of the Ciardi translation
hit the wood.
It was a tremendous moment

for forgetting centuries of literature. The rain
streamed in sheets across the glass. One girl
claimed the whole world
was getting scrubbed in a carwash.

Mr. O Runs a Loose Ship

Students choose any seat they want.
Some sit on the floor, or positioned
on the counter, lean back against
the windows. They eat from sack
lunches, drink tea, water, lattes.
The teacher is a round man
who sits at his desk, twisting to see
who has arrived in time for roll.
He has considered jumping ship
and floating with the current to shore.
Already, his legs are dangling
over the gang rail. He is reminded
that loose ships don't always sink
but they do take on a lot of water.

Name on a Napkin

I walk into the teacher's lounge. Someone has
written *Hey Al* on a brown napkin and left it

lying on the table. I'm curious about who is
messing with me. I respond, *Hey Yourself* in red.

Back at my desk, I let Emily Dickinson
fall open in my lap. The first lines I read,

*My holiday shall be
That they remember me*

and I recall how St. Francis, opening
his book three times,

searched for direction—grey clouds
crowding Rome, a sparrow on a fence,

the poverty of snow. His faith in roulette
is much greater than mine. I settle for one

divination from Amherst—*Hey Yourself*
behind the hedge, I know your name.

Some Roads Don't Go

One afternoon I'm looking
for a roadmap at the Convenience.
The woman at the register
is busy with another customer. I can't
get her attention. Then I find
a Rand McNally. It's dusty,
dated 1961. I point this
out to her at the register.
She asks 10 bucks.
She says it's gently used, mint
condition, a collector's item.
Some of those roads, and she
points to one, blue and wiggly,
don't even go anymore.
She also sells beef jerky
made by Tony out back. I
open the jar and pile some
on Topeka. She says,
all I need to do is drive
down past the river
and take a right. I-70
can't be missed.
She asks where I'm from.
I lie—tell her Amsterdam.
For some reason I
don't want my footsteps
traced. I also hate
lying and I'm starting
to feel something for
her. She deserves better,
something like the truth.
I change my story. She
tells me she wants out
expansively, but has a son
and no money. I can't tell

if she means out of the
Convenience or out of Kansas.
She looks at my hand still
in Topeka. I wiggle my
finger, gold wedding
band glittering, the creases on
my life line
like roads that don't go.

Fox on Greenway Lane

Sometimes I think of the fox I trapped, pissing
out his relocation in the hardwoods. Will he
lope back to 87ᵗʰ Street to hunt the parking lot
behind the Baptist Church? Will he scavenge

scraps behind the Hy-Vee? I thought the old road
out of the city was fair—Kill Creek running north
toward the Kaw, sheltered by walnuts and pin oaks,
the shade and the sun negotiated by cloud.

I must have a narrow view of wildness—having read
too many books on edible plants. I can start a fire
with flint and steel. Seldom lost, I mark each day
of my passing with a knife, each slash

in the post—as sequential as sanity. The fox
trots east toward Greenway, worrying passage
along the creek bed, toward the cul-de-sacs
and drainage pipes—where he steals dog food,

skulks trash trucks, leaps a wilderness of chain link.

Thumpin' Algiers

I.

Easy Money slurps his cherry snowball,
the Crescent slipping behind the *No
Smoking* sign. He's got the mirrored
lenses on—tips a cigarette to his lips,

the curve in the Ray-Bans—off Canal
to Esplanade, hard to port.
Head-on is Algiers, pungent with
the west bank—gardenia,

oleander, myrtle & rose.
It's a soupy sky, man, the Crescent
mildewed like a hymnal, all hopped
with tattoos of rain. Blind

Tony shines in the middle
of Delaronde, jaunty in black
shoes & pin striped suit.

II.

He taps his cane into Algiers—bright
oiled porches, shuttered windows—
front doors pressed
shut with a thumb, sealed like jars.

Every thirty minutes the ferry runs.
Muddy on the move, churning yellow
in diesel fumes. Gulls dive, bitching
at the heat; they steal crepes—sweetened

with jam. A string of green bottles
nods in the ferry's wake, trotline swell,
fish hooks hanging for cat—stink bait,
gut rolled into balls. River wind

funnels between decks—across
the fender-slick Porsche, the fruit truck,
Du Monde's beignets.

III.

The tupelo is hollow, growling
with bees—comb honey. It's all
food of some sort, mudbugs, nutria,
squab on a spit. Like the blues

the gulf rises to the levy, a minor chord
with a repetitive hook, a dollar in a cup,
a drink in the fist. A blind man
swims in flood, dog paddling circles,

pushing off, kicking free, avoiding
sawyers, the trash drift. Maybe
he learned this from a parent
who in lifting him up by the arms

tossed him into Pontchartrain
to swim baby, watched him bob, a little
tug on the homegrown hemp.

Wedding on a Village Street

after Chagall

A man and a woman ride a rooster from
the town where they were born. The groom
wraps his arms around the bride's shoulders.
She has trouble catching her breath—
her wedding shawl as white as the rooster
that carries them. It is evening, the sky
indigo, the moon like a finger nail. In early
summer there is little fear of the days
growing short, or the nights, not being
long enough. The lovers believe no one
has known passion before this moment,
so deep with falling. Already, the rooster
plans for morning. The world rises
in the east with a clutch of forget-me-nots.

Morning Groans Like a Roofer

Another night of trains, I am
sleepless like a moth. Each thought
pushes me from dark shadow
to glowing bulb. I listen in
the quiet hours for a distinct
voice—one that will speak
through the clatter of boxcars,
but the morning has big shoulders.
It broadens in the east, strong from
lifting, hoisting asphalt shingles
up ladders, the sun
splitting the roof like the two
sides of the moon. Even the traffic
muscling onto the interstate,
groans up the freeway ramps.

Cemetery as Dog Park

Sunday afternoon—a cold gray nips
the air—the same gray that drove us
as boys to the cemetery, where sheltered
in the evergreens, protected from the wind,
we planned our futures, one dog
or another panting at our feet. Fifty
years is a long time for boys, an impossibility
for dogs, a big nothing for the sun. Even
the cold, creeping slowly into our thighs,
is as temporary as juniper berries, bagworms,
sprawling limbs. Memory comes and goes
as we count the winters, the dogs that
licked their balls, chewed our shoes,
ran into traffic like happy fools.

III. Returning the Artificial Tree

Returning the Artificial Tree

So I hand her my receipt for
the artificial tree and I say
maybe you can tell me the best
way to do this, and she says
without taking the paperwork—
Let's see, you bought this tree
before the sale, and now you
want to return it, and then
buy it back at the sale price.
And I said yes, I guess you read
my mind. She grinned, you'll
save so much, her fingers
flying through the numbers.
When the transaction was complete
and I had pocketed my 20%
in crisp bills, I patted her on the
arm and said that I liked
the way she did business.
It's just common kindness
she replied, and I waved goodbye,
stepping between the empty
orange carts, the stack of 2 x 4's,
and the box of ten penny nails.
This will pay for my grandkids'
carriage ride through the Plaza
tonight. I considered returning
with an invite: turkey first
at my daughter's, the
clop clop of the horse, then
a photo by the fountain.

Outside the English Department I Lock My Keys in My Car and Realize I Have No Inclination to Be Anywhere

Luckily, it is a bright November day
and the orange leaves outside the English
Department are falling like lazy sparrows.
The officer from campus security is a tall
blonde woman. She's never met
a door she couldn't unlock. I ask her
if she knows how to spell dumbass.
She grins, what's your name? She pries
the door open a quarter of an inch, jams it
with a plastic wedge. Then she begins
fishing into the cab with a long metal rod.
I can't recall but it's either pink or green
and bent and twisted from long use.
With the hook on the end she slowly
turns the window handle. She leans against
the vehicle, the reflection
of the orange leaves and the lazy sparrows
begins to sink into the frame of the door,
my Starbucks cooling in the cup holder.

Ms. W Explains Roethke to AP English

Even if they'd seen a waltz, they'd never
danced one. Oh, they knew the word, like we might
know the words pan flute or bacchanalia. So when I heard
Ms. W's fifth hour go dumb as wall paste,
the definition vague and untendered, I stepped
into the classroom and held out my arms.
She took my left hand, and I slipped my right
around her back (keeping safe distance);
we began to waltz the room. At first bumping
into desks, the trash can, a computer printer,
then finding space, built into a rhythm that allowed
the 123 123 to swing. The class laughed, as we laughed,
a moment of clowning turned graceful, one
they'd recall in posts and tweets.
But for Roethke, I said as we stopped,
and I brushed one student's desk free of books and papers,
his father had been drinking. He slammed
into the world with a belt buckle.
Ms. W stepped onto my shoes, and I would have
careened around the room, as if with my daughter,
except that I couldn't lift my feet. Give him
your sober countenance, she said, as we bent
and swayed in imitation, one that
cannot unfrown itself. Some got the point,
staring at their knuckles on the page.

Writing Every Day

The cat woke me this morning
meowing for breakfast. I tossed
him out the backdoor without
much of a second thought. I dislike
responding to his plaintive whine
so early in the morning—
it only serves to reinforce
his jump-to-my-call behavior.
I wanted a few minutes
to sit before the blank page
and to see what would spill forth,
and I guess this is it. A dumb
story about a dumb cat.
I will write every day—the drill.
Tomorrow, I will fix the toilet.
I understand flappers, plastic floats,
and after flushing, how to wiggle
the chain free from the handle.

Waiting for Word on a Friend's Health on a Night with Crepe Myrtle

Nothing else is fired with bloom
in August, except the memory I have
of you tossing a baseball

high into Sander's elm; ricocheting,
the ball drops unseen through the branches
to an outfield of boys below,

each vying to make the catch, searching
the branches, the leaves, the round shadow—
circling under the ball by sound alone.

And now this cell phone erupts, blinds me
in the darkness, it's blue screen
brighter than the moon, the myrtle—

the blood inside an eardrum.

The Story I Didn't Tell

I'd been laying foundation, digging
the footing for subsidized housing. My father,
afraid that I wouldn't make tuition,

used his connections. The foreman lived
with whiskey at a local motel; he showed me
how to cut thumb-thick rebar with bolt loppers,

how to use the pick to break clay, how
to put my weight into the shovel.
He disliked me immensely. That's how it was.

If I made it to college, I could stay
out of Vietnam. Nonetheless, I got fired
after a few days, and spent the summer

drinking three dollar a case Busch, and
watching Fat Jerry cannonball from a pickup bed
into East Quincy Pit. I made tuition later

with a crowbar and sledge hammer, a new boss
saying simply—gut the place.
Tonight, watching your class line up

at the stage, I picture myself in black robes,
mortar board sliding like cheese
off a pizza, the vowels in my name

rolled like a loose joint between Nelson
and Palmer. I'm certain I wasn't happy,
just ready, like you, for the something

different we were promised.

Opium

3 p.m.

Rain hangs over Cherokee County.
A boy with a sleeveless shirt
steps from the weight room, swaggers

easily across the parking lot,
his arms pumped like two clouds.
Far to the south the tree line

is held in mist. The rolling hills
fold one layer over the next.
A school bus chugs up the blacktop,

a face in each window, peering
into the woods, the tangled weekend,
vines and bracken, stories

told to frighten children.

3 a.m.

The cool air eases into the room
like the suggestion of sex, erotic
as the poppy's paste—the night's

funk, feral as a deer, buck in the sumac,
rut-felt, antler velvet. A light in the back
bedroom—he reads Heinlein, Asimov,

Bradbury. A motorcycle on Rouse,
a faraway train—the quiet trees
spread like umbrellas on the lawn.

Indian summer—moths tap the screen,
resin-coated wings beating wire mesh,
the flashing cherries of the police

a mile out on Highway 7.

Syllabus Change

Cracks of afternoon light slip through the blinds.
Finding Forrester plays on the DVD
while graduating seniors sneak

tweets on their smart phones. They cradle them
in their laps like fragile birds, dropping
bits of daydream into their open beaks.

The teacher has struck the last essay from the syllabus.
Sometimes it is lesson enough
to sit in the darkness with a movie, the familiar

hands of the clock jerking toward the bell.
One boy types the hashtag *timidlyinvincible*.
Another hurries through a worksheet for General Astronomy.

It is not too late to do the math, to triangulate stars,
to press a painted hand to the senior wall.
Outside a flatbed truck has backed up to the curb.

The driver unwinds a hose from the water tank
and begins to soak the newly planted,
the small potatoes, the upstarts.

Lennon and McCartney on Santa Fe Road

The boomers return to the roadhouse
to dance to the Beatles. They gyrate through
"Twist and Shout" and "Day Tripper."
Few manage the floor for more than two
or three songs. They return to their canned beer,
flushed, sucking air like tread-millers
after a cardiac exam. There are moments
in the blue neon when they glimpse each other again,
sweating to an electric guitar, the thump
of the Ludwig, the band superimposed
against a newsreel of missiles—rising
like poems from submarines.
These were the children, hidden below
school desks, arms folded above their heads
in a looping number 9. They dance
hard tonight to the old songs, the highway
through the bean fields winding homeward
between "Let It Be" and "Imagine."

Basement Storage

Sherri organizes boxes in basement storage. Late
this afternoon she still scrapes and knocks them
across the concrete floor. She manages to pitch
a plastic bin of wool sweaters, used when
we climbed Mount Massive, another of blue
rain gear from college football, but a tower of books
that neither of us have looked at this century
stops her. Books are impossible to throw away,
so she stacks them one upon the other. I tell her
Francis Bacon wrote something to the effect
that we build upon each generation's ideas.
Newton said that he stood on the shoulders of giants.
So these old worn pages become landmarks
in basement storage. Certainly, she can unload
some of them—maybe a *College Algebra,*
a water-stained *Riverside Shakespeare,* or
The How to Repair Small Engines. I don't dig deeper.
The ABCs of Beekeeping may be important someday
after I've salvaged the old hive from Terry's farm
and power washed it. Bees can return. Like a forgotten
notion they may swarm around the dogwood limb
that taps the window. They may need rescue
in the suburbs. I don't particularly care for honey
in tea or on toast; it's more like I enjoy the idea
of honey, sweet and dripping in the supers, boxed
for whatever bitterness may arise.

Daddy's Car

Five a.m. in the cold—
a girl warms the Cherokee
before emptying the remaining
Xanax down her throat.
She doesn't want to fall
asleep shivering, ice crystals
up her nose. She wonders
if she has enough gas
to keep the motor
running. She depends
on the car, the reassuring
timing of the engine, the heater
on full, even a little
light from the dash.
It would ruin everything
if the car died, the engine
pinging as it cooled
to silent steel.

Blue Moon Diagnosis

Surprisingly warm in October—
I mow my father's grass, running
the edge of the mower in circles

around the flower beds,
the Madonna, the martin houses.
The deck is cluttered

with pool toys, baskets of
browning petunias. An ideogram
for wisdom lists from a nail.

The above-ground pool has a spiral
of sycamore leaves floating along
the bottom. I strip to my boxers

and swim after them, bringing up
dark handfuls. Shivering, I pull
what's left toward me. The more

I swim, the more the leaves recede
in the vinyl blue
moon beyond my fingertips.

The Empty Branch

There's a moment some mornings when I don't
long for more. I can't plan my day around it,
but it shows up, suddenly like a lover's email.
I might be staring out the rear window
watching the bare-limbed lilac twitch in the wind
and a bird the size of a kestrel will land.
He is out of place in the suburbs, fit for the fencerow,
the looping power lines. He folds his wings
and goes quiet. However, usually it's when
I'm in transition, moving from the truck
to the house, or from the bedroom to the stairs,
when just for a moment, there's a folding of wings—
nothing more to wish for. Of course, it's fleeting,
and as soon as recognized, flies.

piano music

too cold to step outside
period...spring break, no
lesson plans, no desire except

to roll over, wake after 10,
warm coffee, read email,
tweak resignation, eat

leftover noodles & 3 stale
oreo cookies, let the cat
out, check obituaries...

return to the bedroom
thickened, dull stomach, head
fogged...chew tobacco,

spit in a plastic coke
bottle, daydream
about a great poem...

feel guilt about
sins of omission...would
adderall help,

too lethargic to add
capital letters or correct
punctuation, comma

splices connect
without metaphor, ellipsis
follows ellipsis...

a birdsong
in a cage...a piano
pushed north

across wooden
floors...applause from
crickets, an iced-in

fug

On a Motorcycle Too Heavy for Trails

I negotiate the washouts, the crumbling

shoulders—the city noise a distant airplane. Early
leaf change splatters the tops of the trees—notebook
yellow, bag brown, muffler rust. The breeze is

cool, the sun warm. My phone vibrates, reminding
me of a recent commitment in Westport, cancelled
for lack of a better word. I'd rather sit along

the Union Pacific and listen to the woodpeckers,
the insistent cricket, the crows. The yellow susans,
the white yarrow, scattered across the rocks, bloom

even in October. They snag the thin soil with
tenacious roots. They wait the occasional rain, follow
the sun, unpruned, cultivated by wind. Hawks

ride the thermal currents off the bluff. Crows
like iron finials—perch in the bone-white sycamore.
There is time enough for everything—

late bees traffic in sun.

January Moth

Yesterday, a moth flew through the open door
and tapped the light over the sink. January—
touch and go for a moth—even house-bound,
the cold climbs onto his wings. Already, he is less
than he was, ridden by the window's draft—
the brief warm spell ended, blinds shut.
I balance the old wall clock, wind the mainspring
and give the pendulum a push. It ticks through
the night and into the following week. The front
blows so hard that the windows flex like plastic
sheeting. My wife grades essays; her reflection
quivers with each gust, her bathrobe pulled
high to the nape of her neck. The cat nests
between the papers for 3rd and 4th hours.

Corpse Pose

Faculty meeting: I lock my door, turn out the light, and
close my eyes on the floor.

There was a colleague
who used to nap during her planning period.
She was old and tired. I kept an eye
on the clock for her, making sure that she
was up five minutes before the bell. She said,
she needed "recomposed
                    before she decomposed."

Students start to swarm the hallways;
one rattles my doorknob.
I wonder if my feet are visible, sticking out
from under my desk like a body under
a dumpster. Will the school nurse burst
into the room with the Resource Officer?
How do I explain this yoga corpse
during a faculty meeting?

But no one comes,
and that in itself is a lonely thought.
I unlock the classroom door, high five
the first students through.

The Lawyer and the Spider

A friend has a photograph posted
on facebook by his wife. He is unshaven,
his brow furrowed, studying something

on the table. Just behind him, a large
garden spider hangs over his head.
She posts, *should I tell him,* and I imagine

he'd trade the spider for the web
of legal work in front of him. They are
both sticky, involve nearly invisible

strings. Even though both are spun
by masters, the latter at night below
a thumbnail moon, the first behind

closed doors, a web of words
more quotidian than mosquitos. Then again,
his Italian wife might

have moved his chair like a prop,
arranged beside his coffee a catalogue
from Bass Pro, or a new copy

of *Coping with Arachnophobia.* Maybe, it's
a list of projects she has polished,
and just before he can declare honey-do

bankruptcy, she'll leap up and save him
from the spider, then too, she may
wait until he counters, pushes back his chair

to object.

Mr. Charles Shovels Snow at His Mother's Empty House

Tossed with salt, the pavement

blues up like a vein in the wrist.
The house wears a hairdresser's cut—
newspaper cancelled, mail re-routed, lights

timed to follow her make-believe journey—
kitchen to bedroom, bedroom to bath,
somnolent, blank as Ambien.
The furniture sits as was left, chairs pushed

to the Formica table, digital photos
flashing smiles below the clock, the television
clicking on at six, off at ten—

the philodendron watered.

Water in the Streets

I.

Valet attendants jog the sidewalk,
keys in hand, their red shirts clinging
like abandoned newspapers. A leaden

Neptune raises his trident from a fountain.
Big screens splash the World Cup at Chubb's.
A taxi slows in front of Houston's—

a curtain of rain

sprays from the tires to the curb. The driver
pulls into the gutter, front wheels snug
against the sidewalk. A couple dashes

to the cab, the girl lifting her legs and sliding
easily into the backseat. Her friend ducks after her,
both are laughing into their cellphones.

II.

On Saturday night, the tough kids from Prospect
mill along the sidewalk from the Cheesecake Factory
to the theater. They search the street for something

they know, congregate like gunshots in an alley.
They push, strike out at one another, gangly reflections
in the windows of boutiques. The streets

have a price tag. Tourists sip Starbucks,

lick circles around double dips of Haagan-Dasz.
The yellow taxis are replaced—police
angled in intersections. The heat has baked

the streets all evening, roping the flower
beds with crime tape. The promise of more rain
falls through the lights like batons.

III.

The water in the street runs into Brush Creek,
landscaped with pools and water falls, gondolas
rocking likes buoys. Street musicians

tune their guitars on the corner. One of them
recalls how the creek cut a narrow channel
into the Pendergast spillway. Now the current

mirrors the art gallery.

Last week a heron landed, balanced briefly
on one thin leg before winging east. He knows nothing
of oxygen levels, ecoli, or demarcation.

His wings pump like the triangle of a bellows,
a photo op of the city at dusk—
embers of light heating up along the Parkway.

Easter Rabbits

The dog didn't return that night,
but I knew she would eventually,
the rabbits too fat and easy to resist.
I opened the bedroom window,
watching until the gray dawn bled
across the sky. My daughters slept.
I reinforced the hutch wire
and nailed another 2 x 4 across
the door. Each time I fed them, I had
to use the claw and pry off the scab
two-by. Their turds no longer escaped
to the pile on the ground. Some
stuck between the layers of mesh
and rubbed off on their feet.
They sat in their crock bowls
and spilled their water. They grew
fat and lazy. One developed a goiter
the size of a dog's nose. Both
sniffed the air, twitched
while they waited
for something coming.

IV. Paper Birds Don't Fly

Paper Birds Don't Fly

Last night I had a dream
that my father, six years
dead now, left me a message
folded into some kind of origami bird.
He left another for my sister.
I guessed since we were the oldest
of his children, he had
expected us to join him sooner.
There was a girl in the dream,
maybe a younger sister, maybe
a little dead girl sent as a messenger.
I don't know how these things worked.
Sitting at the table with the paper birds,
she unfolded mine and began to read.
I couldn't make out a word
she was saying. I took the note
from her hand and his handwriting blurred
like a camera lens losing focus.
I woke in frustration, trying to will
myself back into sleep
into the dream of my father
where I was sure he'd tried
to cross over
like he had so many times
when he was living.

Whitman's Varied Carols

The toilet flushes. Someone
taps what sounds like a plastic
cup on the concrete floor.
Intermittent. Without rhythm.
A door opens. Closes. Chain
latches. Brass on brass. There
is no thermostat. April begs
warmth. I put on my jacket,
my pants. Pull the blanket
higher. Two pillows, one
blanket. Bed the size of
a boy's. The city that never
sleeps. Walked up from East
Village tonight. Poems tucked
in my satchel. Unsold books
tugging like an anchor. One
old man asleep on the side-
walk. Fatigue jacket. Daffodil
hoodie. Another slumped
over his begging cup. Greased
hair dangling nearly to
the concrete. The shapeliest legs
on 1ˢᵗ Avenue skirt the curb,
boyfriend's arm
draped over her shoulder.
Do not run he asks. Do not turn
to smoke. Both in black. Everyone
in black. Everyone moving
like in an artery—blood cells
racing towards a heart,
pulsing below
a fragile sternum—the city's
breast bone fortified
with tacos, falafel, hummus.

Crayon Sucker

Even as a boy
he took issue with good advice.
Frequently, his teachers
kept a desk for him up front
near the chalkboard. His classmates
expected entertainment.
He ate their enthusiasm.
He rehearsed funny faces at himself
in the mirror, sucked on
purple crayons like cigars,
ate paste from a gallon jar,
construction paper from the top
of his desk. He drew pictures
of great battles on the back of his
math assignments, complete
with sound effects, bombs, missiles,
machine guns, soldiers screaming.
At conferences, the counselor
said he was a real people person.
Teachers regaled his untapped potential.
His parents learned to accept Cs
from their above average,
crayon sucking child.

Poor Girl

              This morning
she is lifted from bed
at the rest home.
She is walked between aides
to the recliner, salvaged
from her house. She parses
out her breakfast
to the drone
of a television, fastened
like a photograph
on the wall. She cannot
change the channels
or adjust the volume,
the remote control a whirl
in dementia's cloud—
her small jug of water
sits on the nightstand
with her dentures, Kleenex,
and Hallmark Love Yous.
The tin of French cookies is
too hard to open; the poinsettia
drops leaves.

After the Book Release Party, Wally Walks Down 39th Street with a Box on His Head

For a moment, he is the only
one on the street, then a waitress
steps out of Jazz
and lights a cigarette. Her smoke
jets skyward into the falling snow.
He tells her there is a poem in this
and he waves his free arm
into the silence of snow.
She lifts her chin in recognition;
the smoke curls from her
lips into her nose. To his myopic eyes
snowflakes streak the sky
like an impressionist's brush strokes—
shops closed, neon smudged like
daubs on a pallet. The gray slush
is slick underfoot. If he falls,
volumes of unsold poems
will spill to his feet.
One of them is a sonnet
about his mother at the nursing home.
In fourteen lines he tells
how she remembers him, or at least,
someone similar to him,
who grew old and blank
and one winter night walked
off behind the 7-11
and forgot to return.

Death Star Halloween

for William Trowbridge

The Death Star Complex was one big party.
My wife and I walked from apartment
to apartment for free drinks. Yoda
shook an 8 ball and reversed his syntax
in the elevator. We drank Cilona Death
Sticks from long, colorful tubes.
They were distributed by Slythmongers
like Pando Baba and Jabba the Hutt.
Later, Princess Leia slapped an ape
in a Chewbaca Goes Down t-shirt. It was
a full blown trick or treat fiasco.
I clicked on my light saber, swinging
like a real bad ass in my Darth Vader mask.
We returned to our apartment; the kitchen
vibrated with crazies from the Cantina.
The Ewoks appeared with plastic
jack-o-lanterns and uninspected candy.
We dumped it on the Millennium Falcon
bedspread and left them to squabble and sort.
I took three Advil and drank a bottle
of Evian. A band of Jedi
begged for a nightcap. I considered
two fingers of my cheapest,
but ended up giving them a hand.

War Trophy

When Mr. Madden wheeled his bright
Pontiac into the driveway,
we were on the roof of his house—

faces pressed to the window.
The house was an irresistible trespass
buried in the trees like a pillbox.

Madden wouldn't kill us (only our fathers
had that right), but he would
gun us down with his salt-filled

12 gauge. Joey (they said) had been
blown spread eagled into
a barbed wire fence. It had taken

days for his blisters to heal.
No one denied it. There were rumors—
of skulls, Nazi helmets, splendid

daggers, an Iron Cross.

Old Madden, one leg on the floorboards,
the other planted in gravel, shook
his fist like a club. Wally and I jumped—

parachutists with knees bent,
rolling into Normandy. My brother,
only six, wept as he struggled

down the ladder. On the roof where
I had pushed my nose to the glass,
I'd seen an end table with a lamp,

an embroidered doily, and
a framed black and white
of a woman with a girl and a dog.

My brother lost his shoe as we fled.
The old man turned it in his hand.
He lobbed it after us, a grenade

like we'd seen in the movies.

Sticks and Stones

I do not attend the theater
without my bomb sniffing dog.

I purchase a second ticket,
offer him popcorn, his own

box of jujubes. Together,
we spring for a laugh

in the safe darkness. I scratch
behind his ears. He presses

his nose for disaster
into the palm of my hand.

There are other men and women
in the rows ahead. Some

have dogs, some wear Kevlar.
All are trained in broken bones.

William Blake Saw Angels in a Tree

I saw a panda in the yard this afternoon.
When I looked closer, it turned out to be
a patch of melting snow.
My vision has been failing for weeks,

glaucoma, cataracts, retinal edema.
A few years ago a deer hunter claimed
a black bear lumbered out of the woods
near Arcadia. He saw another

on the highway to Baxter Springs. That
was one too many. A friend
built a mountain lion trap
baited with deer meat. He caught a really

large dog. In southern Missouri
the Spook Light dances on dirt roads,
an anomaly of phosphorous and Indian
legend. It's seen best after a good rain

when the bell oaks are dripping
and the creeks swell with rumors of flood.
A Boy Scout troop saw its blue glow
stretch the entire width of Hornet Road.

It was so bright they could count the rocks
scattered from shoulder to shoulder.
One boy said his shoes started to smoke.
When I was a kid, a good friend claimed

to see an alligator in Pittsburg, Kansas.
Even after the sheriff reported an escape
from a nearby reptile farm, my parents
refused to let me play with him.

Diamond Princess T-Ball

Mothers and fathers walk their children
to the edge of the playing field. They unfold
canvas chairs and sit on the berm overlooking

the diamond. Traffic from the highway is muted.
Trains in the distance blow long horns
at unseen crossings. Young ball players take

practice swings on deck. They chew bubble gum
and wear oversized batting helmets.
Meadowlarks lift in song from fence posts.

The deep blue sky covers the earth—everyone bats,
everyone runs the bases. No one is ever
called out on strikes. A little girl guzzles

the water bottle she has rescued from the dirt.
Her game shirt reads *Diamond Princess,*
untucked, it stretches to her knees. Tomorrow

takes care of tomorrow, time for strike outs,
errors at short, right field.

Off Broadway

I roll down my window
and hand the leading lady a five.
She has wonderfully
sad eyes, humble and downcast,
her rehearsed blues
working the traffic. She steps
off the exit ramp onto a metal
utility cover, bows her head
and begins to move her lips.
She lifts her eyes—as if
to speak a second line—but approaches
another fogged windshield.
The driver cracks his glass,
waves the price of admission.
She returns to her spot, lowers her head,
and speaks inaudibly into her coat.
When the light changes, I drive
north onto Broadway. Her ritual
on the manhole cover
stays with me, the slush on her
boots melting—the scam—
if that's what it is—
relevant theater.

Carrying a Knife

Mom showed me how to carry
a knife safely, out to the side,
with the blade against a leg.
I practiced with a butter knife,
tight roping the kitchen linoleum
from sink to refrigerator.
It didn't seem possible to fall—
the knife plunging like a heron's beak.
When no one was watching, I took
Dad's fish knife, and turning the blade
to my stomach, tested the entire width
of the backyard. My body tingled
with the breathing of it, point to shirt.
I began to run, knife bouncing
against cotton. I leapt the iris bed
into the open street, only then
did I notice a berry of blood
barely enough to remember.

Marbles

I owned a Wrist Rocket that could thump
marbles against the barn roof. I was told
it could take down rabbits and squirrels.
My parents saw it as a hedge against rifles
so they let me order it from the catalog.
One Sunday I hunted the backyard
with a pocketful of marbles.
I hit trash cans and telephone poles, popped
paint buckets into surrender behind the tool shed.
Finally, I aimed at a blue jay, drew the rubber
surgical hose to my chin. The jay
exploded before my eyes. His insides
strung like spaghetti in the wet grass.
Immediately, I wanted to put him back together,
slip his stomach back into his feathers, send him
back to what he was before.
Instead, I lifted him with the tip of a shovel
into a small hole in the neighbor's beans.
I stuffed the sling in a drawer. That night
I slept facing the wall, the only hole
I could find big enough for a boy.

Old Glenn's Story

I hid in the boxcars
across the road, close
to where we buried Flop
the black dog. My aunt
who had taken up with Henry
during hard times let me
slip out the backdoor
when his mood turned dark.
She said come back
when the light's out,
after the "alone time."
Henry ran a few head of cattle
in the scrub pasture
between the tracks and the road.
I bucked his hay bales
and broke his ice in January.
He taught captivity.
I wore his cigar bands
on my middle finger, but his smoke
stole into every soft cushion
in the house. In June
he tied a forked branch
around a calf's neck
to keep it from straying
between loose strands of barbed wire.
My aunt sold the cow on the sly.
She stuffed the money
in her get-away tin.
The new owner came at night
after she'd snapped
the yoke branch and left the pieces
tangled in fence.

The Five Geese Death Poem

1

You butchered a goose,
wings spread on a chopping block.
An old woman in a scullery cap
plucked by the fistful. She worked
without a word to you, dipping
the bird into a boiling pot.
Your grandchildren danced among

the feathers, splitting the wishbone,
sopping bread into grease bowls
with their small, wet fingers.
You walked the narrow streets
with your hands in the air,

2

honing your death poem.
The goose, a dream symbol,
part of a perfectly ironic
5-7-5 haiku—a blade
at the throat of sentimentality.
At bedside

you scratched each syllable
on a debit card receipt, still rich
with the wood-smoked sauce
from last night's ribs—
another cliché, another rub.
You sat with the pencil

3

in your teeth and remembered
rising to honking geese
in October, leaping from bed
before your parents, pounding
after the noisy V, shoes
like clubs in the wet grass—
the domed skull of a puffball

kicked into a cloud of spores.
You pumped your BB gun
into the sky, wings everywhere
over the neighbor's maples—
the yellowed oak

4

a reminder to gather
before winter. You pictured
the cardboard racer, perched
like a goose wing at the top
of the overpass. The faster
you pushed, the more pieces flew
into the street—corrugated fenders,
newspaper hood, broomstick

steering. Two skinny bird dogs
ran inside the neighbor's fence—
incisors slicing the air, muscles
shouldering the chain link.

5

You climbed the ladder to paint
the eaves of your house, the timbre
of children's voices in flight
above the playground. They were
not unlike geese. You dipped
your brush into the bucket,

feathering the excess paint
from the tip of the bristles.
There was always more
than you could reach, goosed
at the top of the ladder,
leaning into the sky.

The Handyman Drinks

in the shade of a sweet gum.
His saw is plugged into an orange
extension cord which is fed
through the storm window
and into the house. Hammer,
nails, tool belt are scattered
like leaves on the new porch.
Miller Lite bottles
shine with a dull amber
around his feet. The beer
has gone down too easily, one
after the other. He loads
the scrap lumber into the
back of his truck and drives
home on dirt roads—
Kansas sun angled through
the trees, strip pits lush
and overgrown in
drunken green. He drives fast,
eating carry-out chicken,
tossing the bones out the window
like pleasant abstractions,
road dust a billowing curtain.
He stops at a jeep trail
slanted over a slag dump, eroded
and rutted from neglect.
He unloads tongue-and-groove
and ripped two-by-fours. He pitches
them with the beer bottles
into a tangle of briar. Cicadas
build in the deepening woods.

Asphalt

The road crew hired temps
between semesters
to stand beside the hopper
shoveling. The foreman
disliked college students.
He never learned our names,
referenced us by the tools
we carried—Skip and I
were Shovels, scraping the hot
mix into the conveyor.
Ronnie the college drop-out
advanced to Rake.
He followed the paver,
flicking the screed ridge
to a smooth seam.
All summer I shoveled the city
streets, made-do with whatever
shade I could catch. Each day
at five, we cleaned the tools
with diesel and putty knives.
Then we sprayed our boots,
kicking our steel toes against
a bar of rail line. We wet rags
with the diesel and scrubbed
our hands and faces.
Then I drove home, a towel
on the seat, another on the arm rest.
I hung my work clothes
on the fence behind the house.
They appeared capable
of walking off on their own.

Mulligan

When I was a kid, my grandmother

used to take me on walks
along the railroad tracks near her house.
After summer storms, branches
littered the rail bed. I used them
as baseball bats. Sometimes
tramps emerged from the dumps,
scarecrows knocking backdoors
for handouts. Grandmother
said they were like deadwood,
pruned by wind. She kept

the door locked, even in the daytime.
They camped, trains in-trains out,
by the clay quarry. Some slept
in the stacks of drainage pipes, others
in brush lean-tos. She wouldn't
walk with me into the hobo jungle.
I had met one close-up before
on the sidewalk outside of the Pla-mor.
He was a bum, but he'd tapped
me on my ball cap with his knuckle,
and said, Hey pal, as he passed.

From the trestle, we watched them
knotted over their orange fire, sharing
mulligan from a coffee can.
Grandmother said, Poor things,
and then she hurried me home.

The Dog at the End of the Day

Some days I want to write my last poem.
one that will manifest the controlling image
of my future silence. It will have to say

it all—like the way a branch bends
with the weight of a bird, and then springs
back in flight. This image needs

to embrace emptiness, the shape left
to absence, the quiet after a mourning dove,
the course of a leaf tailing through rain.

Once I've found this final thought,
I can sit in the yard with a few chickens
and a dog, lazy and well-fed, not too close

to demand my time, but over there
near the birdbath with one eye open.

Acknowledgments

After the Pause: "Sticks and Stones"

Ann Arbor Review: "Water in the Streets"

BOAAT: "Asphalt"

Boston Literary Magazine: "Marbles," "Mr. O Runs a Loose Ship"

The Camel Saloon: "Easter Rabbits," "Hail Mary," "Jack of All Trades Drives Irene to the Hospital"

Camroc Press Review: "The Fifteen Dollar Vacation," "Following Junkyard," "Tony Paces the Sidelines"

Coal City Poetry Review: "Good at What You Do," "Poor Girl," "Popcorn and a Movie," "War Trophy"

Chiron Review: "The Lovely Mechanic"

Drunk Monkeys: "Death Star Halloween"

Eunoia: "Blue Moon Diagnosis," "Bridge Club," "The Dog at the End of the Day," "The Empty Branch," "Name on a Napkin"

Front Porch Review: "On the Morning of My Daughter's 40th Birthday," "The Five Geese Death Poem," "We Sang Dark Songs in Grade School"

The Galway Review: "Almost Michael Corleone," "Diamond Princess," "Forgetting Dante in Third Period," "Martial Arts," "Mickey Mantle as Long Shot," "Midlife Crises"

The Gap Toothed Madness: "Reading Fiction after Midnight," "Some Roads Don't Go," "Dog Poet"

Hermes Poetry Journal: "In Late Winter—the Squirrel"

I-70 Review: "White High Tops"

The Innisfree Poetry Review: "Morning Groans Like a Roofer," "Wedding on a Village Street"

Jellyfish Whispers: "Kansas as Wine Dark Sea"

The Journal, Kansas Leadership Center: "The Last Farm on 87th Street"

Kansas Time + Place: "Lennon and McCartney on Santa Fe Road"

Long Island Quarterly: "Mr. Charles Shovels Snow at His Mother's Empty House," "Unbroken Design"

Lummox: "Corpse Pose"

Melancholy Hyperbole: "January Moth," "The Story I Didn't Tell," "Thumpin' Algiers"

The Ofi Press Journal: "Cemetery as Dog Park"

Poetry Bay: "Whitman's Varied Carols"

Poppy Road Review: "Driving into Lecompton with an Hour to Kill"

Pyrokinection: "piano music"

Rattle: "Paper Birds Don't Fly"

Red River Review: "Basement Storage," "On a Motorcycle Too Heavy for Trails"

San Pedro River Review: "The Handyman Drinks"

Star 82 Review: "Mulligan"

Stone Highway Review: "Steam Engine 1023"

The Subterranean Quarterly: "Dusting Back the Five Year Old," "The Ghost Clara," "Improvisation"

Tar River Poetry: "Ms. W Explains Roethke to AP English," "Outside the English Department I Lock My Keys in My Car and Realize I Have No Inclination to Be Anywhere"

Turtle Island Quarterly: "After the Book Release Party, Wally Walks Down 39th Street with a Box on His Head," "Steps," "The Wind We See"

Up the Staircase Quarterly: "Fox on Greenway Lane"

VAYAVYA: "Opium," "Waiting for Word on a Friend's Health"

Wild Goose Poetry Review: "Swamp Tour," "Taking the ACT"

Wild Quarterly: "Syllabus Change"

Word Riot: "Returning the Artificial Tree"

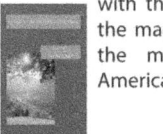
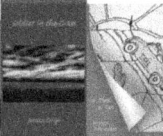

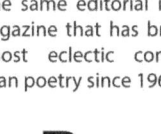

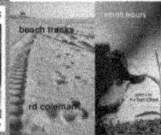

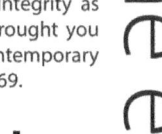